Organize Your Life

How To Organize Your Life, Declutter Your Home And Office, Clear Your Mind And Get Stuff Done!

Lilly Sparks

STOP!!! Before you read any further....Would you like to know the secrets of Anti-Aging?

If your answer is yes, then you are not alone. Thousands of people are looking for the secret to reducing wrinkles, looking younger, and maintaining a youthful appearance.

If you have been searching for these answers without much luck, you are in the right place!

Not only will you gain incredible insight in this book, but because I want to make sure to give you as much value as possible, right now for a limited time you can get full **100% FREE access to a VIP bonus EBook** entitled **Anti-Aging Made Easy!**

Just Go Here For Free Instant Access:

www.LuxyLifeNaturals.com

Legal Notice

Disclaimer Notice

Table Of Contents

Introduction

I want to thank you and congratulate you for purchasing the book, *"Organize Your Life: How To Organize Your Life, Declutter Your Home And Office, Clear Your Mind And Get Stuff Done!"*.

This "Organize Your Life" book contains proven steps and strategies on how to organize every facet of your life – your daily activities, your home, your office, and even your mind!

Included in this book is the information that would help you gain an understanding on the fundamentals of an organized life. This book will not only help you get rid of physical clutter – it would also help you clear your mind and be more organized in various aspects of your life; both in your home and office. You would be introduced to the merits of a minimalist lifestyle, and how to adopt it.

You will as well get to discover some simple steps on how you can easily organize your life so that you won't have to face a stressful day ever!

Thanks again for purchasing this book, I hope you enjoy it!

Chapter 1: Fundamentals Of An Organized Life

What are the characteristics of someone who is good at organizing? There are four fundamental traits which you have to absorb and live by so that you can efficiently organize your life. These are the following:

1. Understand the concept of "enough".

There are only 24 hours in a day, and 7 days in a week. Your body can function for several hours in a day however, you need to take a rest at nighttime. With these physical limitations, you should recognize that you cannot possibly do everything in one day. If you're a student, would you still accommodate your extra-curricular activities knowing that you still have a lot of studying to do? An organized life entails that you have enough time to do every single thing listed in your schedule.

2. Acquire only the necessary things and get rid of the rest.

How will you know which activities should you include in your schedule? For this question, you have to apply the minimalist's philosophy. In minimalism, you give more value to the urgent and important things. Similarly, in organization, you prioritize doing the most important activities while you put the miscellaneous tasks at the bottom of your To-Do list.

3. Create a "simple" schedule.

While it is said that you should only join activities that are within your limits, that doesn't mean that you have to do everything until you reach your limit.

Everyone knows that life isn't a predictable thing. There are times when unexpected events will tear your pre-planned schedule into pieces. Therefore, it is recommended that you only create a "simple" schedule. Aside from putting a manageable workload, you also need to leave an ample wiggle room in your schedule.

4. Constantly revisit your life for improvements.

For every change of resources or environment, you need to examine if there is a need for you to adjust on how you do things. For instance, if you have just bought a new computer, will it have an impact in your daily life? If yes, you should reorganize to accommodate such change.

Although it is said that you should at least learn to imbibe these fundamental principles, you can't possibly change your mindset in a whim by just reading this. In this book, you will learn the possible ways on how you can incorporate these values in your life for the better.

Chapter 2: Secrets Of A Minimalist

As you've learned from the previous chapter, one of the fundamental principles in organization is minimalism. But what is it about? And, why do people need to know about it to be organized?

History of Minimalism

Minimalism describes a style wherein the elements of design are reduced to a minimum. In visual arts, one of the works by a Russian painter named Kasimir Malevich was probably the first art to be considered as a minimalist piece; his 1913 composition comprises only of a black square against a white background.

This philosophy has been applied not only in visual arts but also in other fields such as music, literature, design, and architecture. For instance, in the 1980s minimalist architecture has become popular particularly in London and New York.

Since minimalism embodies simplicity and elegance, many people have taken interest in the movement which has then proliferated in numerous industries. Aside from the sophistication of such style, it strongly conveys the idea that people can live well even with only the barest of necessities.

Virtues of a Minimalist

A minimalist lives by the saying "Less is more." As such, he renounces all the unnecessary things in his life and keeps only what he needs.

In a world where everyone wants to acquire more, a minimalist does the opposite. He recognizes that there is beauty in having less, and that having so much isn't desirable for him.

To better see things in the eyes of a minimalist, here are some examples for you to ponder on. Living in a big house would require you to spend a lot just to maintain it. More toys for the kids meant more litter to clean. Also, having a big wardrobe would make you fret every time because you can't immediately decide on what to wear.

With these things in mind, a minimalist believes that "bigger" doesn't necessarily equate to being "better" and that getting more stuff won't make you happy. Instead, they value quality over quantity. By acquiring only the things that they need and by spending time with their loved ones, a minimalist is able to find peace and joy.

What are the perceived benefits of living the minimalist's way? For one, you will have more freedom in terms of time and finances. And with this freedom, you will be less stressed and pleased with how things are going around you. As such, you will have a better control on every aspect of your life by applying minimalist principles in organization.

Chapter 3: Setting Goals To Become More Organized And How To Achieve Them

Organization starts with having a clear goal in mind. Goals are the things that you want to achieve at the end of a certain activity. For instance, if your major goal is to be the top student at the end of the school year, you need to incorporate tasks in your daily activities that will help you reach that goal.

General Goals

How do you create a goal? Ultimately, your goal should be able to answer the three "W" questions; What, Where and When. As an example, let's say you just got in the Accounting Department of a local bank as an Accounting Assistant. As part of your plans to organize your career, you need to create a goal that will be your guide and come up with this:

- To become an Accounting Manager within the next 5 years

Is your goal comprehensive? You can check that with the "W" questions. In this case, the "What" pertains to you becoming an Accounting Manager. The "Where" is your current company while the "When" is five years from now.

Specific Goals

Most people would opt to create specific goals apart from their major goal. Since the general goal is quite broad in nature, it doesn't really help that much in terms of organization. Therefore, you need to create specific goals based on your general goal.

Given the previous example, your specific goal should look like this:

- Master your current work as an Accounting Assistant within the first year

- Rotate in other areas of the Accounting Department every six months to one year
- Attend seminars and trainings related to Accounting at least once every year
- Be an Assistant Manager after three years
- Train current employees and new hires in the different job areas in the Accounting Department after you have become an Assistant Manager
- Volunteer for the Officer-In-Charge position once the need arises
- Get certifications in the field of Accounting within the period
- Take part in all the company events every year

As you've noticed, the specific goals explicitly state the activities that you need to do in order to achieve your general goal. Similar with your major goal, it also answers the 3 "W" questions that you have used earlier.

In setting your goals, make sure that it is attainable within the time period that you have specified. Using the example above, you can't aim to be a Vice President of the company in just five years of working experience.

In organizing things, having an objective gives you a sense of direction so that you won't be lost on what to do during your planning stage. More importantly, these goals serve as your inspiration to get you going.

Chapter 4: Utilizing A To Do List And Daily Planner

Now that you have successfully plotted your general and specific goals, you may now proceed to organize your life in minute details, or in a day-to-day basis.

To-Do List

To start, you need to establish your To-Do list. This document will enumerate every activity that you need to accomplish during the day.

Again, assume that you're in the shoes of an Accounting Assistant. What are the things that you have to do on a Monday? Here's an example:

September 1, 2014, Monday

Tasks To Do

- Invite officemates to your birthday bash next week
- Read banking news on the internet
- Retrieve data from the bank's branches
- Retrieve data from the other units of the bank
- Attend to all queries sent via email
- Prepare the bank's balance sheet
- Send the balance sheet report to the recipients
- File your vacation leave for the month

According to your list, you have eight activities to do this coming Monday. However, by just looking at your To-Do list, you're not sure which tasks have the higher priority over the others. As such, you may have a hard time figuring out which of these activities you should do first. You also have no idea on how long each task take will because it's not indicated in the To-Do list.

Daily Planner

The limited data in the To-Do list makes it inadequate for your organizational needs. For that reason, it is essential for you to prepare a daily planner alongside with a To-Do list.

If the To-Do list primarily lays down all the activities that you have to do, the daily planner breaks down each of these activities into your working hours. Thus, you will know the tasks that you need to do for each time period. Also, the daily planner indicates the urgency of each task.

Let's integrate the To-Do list above into your daily planner.

September 1, 2014, Monday

Importance – Start time – Activity

High – 8:30 AM – Retrieve data from the bank's branches

High –9:00 AM – Retrieve data from the other units of the bank

Low – 10:00 AM – Break

High – 10:30 AM – Prepare the bank's balance sheet

Low – 12:00 NN – Lunch break

High – 1:00 PM – Prepare the bank's balance sheet

High – 2:00 PM – Send the balance sheet report to the recipients

Low – 3:00 PM – Break

Normal – 3:30 PM – Attend to all queries sent via email

Normal– 4:00PM – Read banking news on the internet

Low– 4:30PM – File your vacation leave for the month

Low – 5:30PM – Invite officemates to your birthday bash next week

Compared to the To-Do list, having a daily planner makes it easier for you to manage your day ahead. You can already see that the activities are segregated into their respective time slots. This gives you confidence that you will be able to finish your most important tasks before the end of the day. Also, through the daily planner you can pace yourself so that you can finish all activities.

Note that you should not consider squeezing as much work as you can in just one day. As seen in the above example, breaks are widely distributed in the whole day. Moreover, not all highly important tasks should be designated in one day. This is so that you won't be stressed and that you will still have energy to survive the whole week.

Chapter 5: Tips To Declutter Your Home

Organizing your life doesn't only entail you to manage your daily activities. Besides that, you should also organize your surroundings so that you can be more efficient in doing things.

One major area which you can organize is your home. This place serves as your refuge after a hard day's work. However, with an untidy home, how can you even relax with all the mess around? Hence, you should aim to declutter your home at least once every month.

Keep Only the Essentials

How can you make your home clutter-free? You will need to apply the basic principle of minimalism to do this. In decluttering, remember that only the essential things should be kept among your possessions. Thus, it follows that the rest should be disposed of.

Decluttering your room starts with identifying all the essential things, or the things that you cannot live without. For example, a cellular phone is something that is indispensable today but having hundreds of clothes isn't.

Therefore, you need to trim down all your belongings aggressively to effectively get rid of all the clutter in your home. Use the checklist below as a guide in segregating the essentials from the non-essentials.

1. Have you used the item within the past six months?
2. If it is a seasonal item (i.e., used during winter seasons only), have you used it within the past year?
3. Will you use it for the next six months?
4. Do you not have a similar item in the house?
5. Is the item still in a good condition?

If you have answered yes to all questions, then that item is most probably an essential one. Based on the checklist above, luxurious items such as antiques or jewelries are considered non-essential.

However, because these items have a significant market value, you can sell them off to an auction store or to a pawn shop instead of throwing them away. Even decors would be non-essential too so make sure to keep only one or two of these items.

One Room at a Time

The art of decluttering also follows an organization of some sort. You cannot possibly declutter all the rooms at the same time; you're bound to forget and lose things in the process. It is recommended that you start with only one room and that you only move along after you have finished in that area.

Once you have decided on a room, make an inventory of all the essentials then eliminate everything that doesn't make the cut. Furthermore, all the things that won't be used on a daily basis should be stored in the cabinet.

Other Tips

As per minimalist principles, your home should only contain accent decorations that are of quality. You don't have to put excessive ornaments in your room. Instead of looking pleasant, it will turn only your area into a crowded mess.

In addition, you should only use plain patterns and subdued colors in your wall. Furniture should be kept minimal especially if there are only a few individuals living in your house.

Having an organized home exudes a calm and soothing atmosphere for its inhabitants. Besides having a more appealing abode, a minimalistic layout makes it easier for you to clean your home.

Chapter 6: Tips To Declutter Your Office

Now that you're done with decluttering your home, you can now proceed to declutter the places outside your house. For those who have a full time- job, it is in their office where they spend most of their day, which explains why the workplace is considered everyone's second home.

With that said, it is important that you declutter your working area in the office. By having a cleaner and more organized workstation, you can improve your productivity by a notch.

Your Physical Desk

This one is probably the most labor-intensive among the three areas that could be decluttered in your office. Rearranging stacks of papers and folders would be quite a daunting task to do in day especially if you've been in your job for a long time.

For that reason, you should expand your cleaning schedule to at least two weeks if you're going to declutter your workdesk. That should give you an ample time to organize things without hurting your day job in the process.

First, you have to identify the basic supplies that you need in your work. Do you really need to have those stacks of paper beside you all the time? How about that figurine, does it serve a purpose at all?

Based on the 5S method of process improvement, you should only keep five things in your desk at all times and that all the other things should be kept hidden from sight. Here is a list of the recommended things that you can put in your desk: a pen (may have a penholder), a tumbler, a mobile phone, a planner, and one decoration (e.g., flower vase) only.

Your Desktop Computer

People just love putting every computer icon in their desktop. They think having all the program shortcuts and documents in that area would make things easier for them. However, the clutter in your desktop only makes it difficult to search for a file. For that reason, you should also apply minimalist principles in your desktop.

To do that, you should keep all the files in their respective folders. As for the programs, pinning their icons in the taskbar would suffice. After this, your desktop should be clear of any obstructions and now you can work seamlessly while enjoying the view of your desktop wallpaper.

Your Email's Inbox

Apart from your desktop, another area in your computer which you usually access is your email. Since email messages are generally saved into remote servers, people don't really care about the space that these messages occupy in their company's database. Most of them opt to keep all their emails in their inbox because they think they would probably need it in the near future.

Unfortunately, as more and more emails are being managed by your inbox, it will eventually result to a slower system. Thus, to be able to efficiently manage your emails, create folders in your email program and store the messages in these folders.

For emails which you think are not quite important, examine if you still need to file them in your folders. For instance, emails about the latest weather bulletin may not be necessary for you if you're working as a sales agent. Through this, you can easily find the emails that you need by deleting the useless ones.

Decluttering your office isn't a one-day event. Therefore, you don't have to pressure yourself into finishing everything in just one sitting. Give yourself enough time for you to organize your work area.

Chapter 7: Mindful Meditation And Organization

With the hectic working conditions in the city, relaxation has most likely become an alien word to you. However, you need to step back and take a breather to ensure your overall health and happiness.

Ask yourself: when was the last time that you took a long vacation? If you can't remember at all, then you might probably be someone who is almost burned out with fatigue. In lieu with that, here are some tips to keep you from being stressed and depressed.

Be Appreciative of What You Have

As mentioned in the first chapter, you should be able to comprehend the concept of enough. Although there is no limit in acquiring stuff, once you understand your basic needs you will know the right amount of belongings that you should have to be able to live well.

It will also help if you will look for people who have been surviving with just a few possessions. You are blessed that you are able to provide for yourself sufficiently. It's now time for you to focus on the more important things in life instead of the material things.

Focus on Doing and not on Buying

As a saying by Democritus goes, "Happiness resides not in possessions and not in gold; happiness dwells in the soul." Indeed, even though rich people have it all, some of them don't really feel happy and contented in their life.

Happiness lies inside of you so it's for you to find out what makes you happy. Don't spend your fortune in material things that will disappear eventually. Instead, spend time with people that you value the most because pleasant memories will last a lifetime.

All in all, these guidelines entail rethinking about your necessities in life. Do you really need a car such that you are willing to burden yourself with its exorbitant costs? Do you still need to transfer to a bigger home when everyone's settled already in your simple yet stress-free neighborhood? Besides a person's basic needs, do you really need anything else to be happy?

Chapter 8: How To Boost Productivity

Productivity refers to the rate at which a person produces an output given the same number of inputs. In the manufacturing setting, this is measured by how many goods a labor can produce in a specified period.

Employers prefer that their workers have higher productivity because aside from producing more output, it is a sign that their personnel are doing their jobs efficiently. Being an employee yourself, how can you increase your productivity at work?

1. Do minor activities straightaway.

Unsolicited phone calls and miscellaneous emails usually present an addition to your daily activities. It is recommended that these minor tasks should be acted upon as soon as possible so that your mind will be free of worry. Also, this avoids menial activities to be piled up, which in turn may disrupt your schedule.

2. Get a "mental break".

You can't possibly sit down all morning in front of your computer to do all your work. This saps out all the energy that you have that you may not be as productive later. Thus, you need to get a "mental break" once in a while.

Stand up and go around the office for a few minutes. Or better, you can just fix your working area in case it gets too congested with stuff. Taking a break recharges your mind. Thus, when you get back to work, you'll become more productive than ever.

3. Save time through technology.

If you think that you can use programs in order to be more productive in your work, then you may do so. An example would be to create a macro so that any repetitive tasks in your spreadsheet program can be done immediately.

4. Turn off the internet.

Facebook, Instagram and other similar sites are a big disruption to your work. Once you get hold of a social media feed, it's hard to get your attention away from it. By turning off the internet, you can never access these sites in your workplace.

With these suggestions, you should be able to work more efficiently than ever. As an employee, being more productive is beneficial for you. Besides being devoid of stress, you may also receive bonuses from your company.

Chapter 9: Stop Procrastination

The worst enemy that you will face in organizing your life is procrastination. Most people are only zealous at the start of the process. However, once they face any difficulty, they tend to divert themselves from addressing these problems. If you want to organize your life, you should avoid this trap at all costs.

Reward System

In order to push their employees to do more, companies use an effective reward system for their personnel. Usually, it is in the form of monetary rewards, but sometimes they use benefits and freebies to boost their employee's productivity.

The same way can be applied to you. You should reward yourself after you have successfully accomplished your schedule for the week without getting swayed off track.

Buddy System

If you're only alone in this venture and have no one to report to, the tendency is for you to slack off. Thus, you need someone who can monitor you in your progress. It is much better if that person shares the same values as you so that you can motivate each other in organizing your life.

Procrastination is indeed a show-stopper for those who want to have a better and organized life. With these steps, hopefully you can effectively incorporate your new routine without going into procrastination.

Chapter 10: Developing Daily Good Organizational Habits And Mistakes To Avoid

Organization doesn't stop from learning how to do it. You should also hone your skills such that you can be better at what you do. This chapter will focus on the ways on how you can further develop your organizational skills.

1. Follow your daily planner.

The daily planner provides you with a general overview of your activities and their corresponding schedules within the day. Besides putting all your tasks in time periods, it focuses on you starting your day with the most important tasks first.

A daily planner serves as the foundation for organization. If you can't push yourself into doing what you have planned to do, then what's the sense of organizing things? You should follow your daily planner by heart so that you can develop a sense of discipline.

2. Make organizing your life a habit.

According to a study by the European Journal of Social Psychology, on the average it takes around 66 days for a person to form a habit. As such, you should practice the organizational principles for at least two months so that you won't be able to go back to an unruly way of life.

3. Prevent yourself from buying non-essentials.

In the televisions, billboards and even in your phone, there are advertisements around. As such, wherever you go, temptations are everywhere. In order to avoid being enticed by these marketing tactics, shun away from accessing media platforms.

For instance, you can install ad blockers in your mobile devices. During sales, don't attempt to go to the mall. Temptation is all in the mind; if you don't let these things reach you, you won't be lured at all.

That ends the first step in your journey towards organizing your life. Learning the ropes is just half of what you need to do; the rest is to act on it now.

Conclusion

Thank you again for purchasing the book "Organize Your Life: How To Organize Your Life, Declutter Your Home And Office, Clear Your Mind And Get Stuff Done!"

I am extremely excited to pass this information along to you, and I am so happy that you now have read and can hopefully implement these strategies going forward.

I hope this book was able to help you understand the principles of organization and how you can apply it in several areas of your life, so that you can be efficient and stress-free always.

The next step is to get started using this information and to hopefully live a wonderful life devoid of any clutter!

Please don't be someone who just reads this information and doesn't apply it, the strategies in this book will only benefit you if you use them!

If you know of anyone else that could benefit from the information presented here please inform them of this book.

Finally, if you enjoyed this book and feel it has added value to your life in any way, please take the time to share your thoughts and post a review on Amazon. It'd be greatly appreciated!

Thank you and good luck!

Preview Of:

<u>Frugal Simplicity</u>

101 Ways To Use Frugal Simplicity For Organizing And Decluttering Your Life And Embracing The Simplicity Lifestyle For Greater Personal Finances And Freedom!

Introduction

I want to thank you and congratulate you for purchasing the book, *Frugal Simplicity: 101 Ways To Use Frugal Simplicity For Organizing And Decluttering Your Life And Embracing The Simplicity Lifestyle For Greater Personal Finances And Freedom.*

Do you know what many successful people have in common? Apart from leading stress-free and happy lives and achieving their goals in life, they have a secret; they value the importance of frugality.

The fact is, dealing with problems such as not having time for family and friends, not having any money during emergencies, and even not having sufficient sleep may often be a result of poor work ethics, poor decision-making, poor habits and poor strategizing. If you think there is no escape out of your messy life, you are wrong. There is a solution, and you can get started by familiarizing yourself with frugal simplicity.

Thanks again for purchasing this book, I hope you enjoy it!

Chapter 1: How To Be Frugal And Save Money

As defined on numerous sites, frugality is about knowing how to live accordingly by not allowing food, money, supplies, and mostly anything to go to waste. Some would argue that it is about fleeing from lavishness and being a cheapskate. Well, it is not. Rather, it is about wisely making the most out of what you have. Should things unfold according to your plans, heaps of joys in the form of self-fulfillment along with financial security are bound to come your way.

1 – Go for the Original

Buy original items, instead of there more affordable counterparts. On occasion, there are necessary purchases including a car tire, faucet, cabinets, and beds. A way to save? Choose the genuine kinds. Usually, they are more expensive but they are cost-effective (i.e. built with quality, minimal maintenance needed and sturdy).

2 – NO to Waste

Use resources wisely. Have you been advised to turn off the lights during the day? How about preparing a glass of water to use when brushing your teeth? Or, replacing your lights to energy-efficient bulbs? The reminders are probably redundant but you have to pay attention anyway. They can be a huge help in reducing the total costs of your monthly utility (electricity, energy, and water) bills.

3 – All You Need Is One (Card)

Consolidate credit and debit cards. Owning multiple accounts costs big so make sure your salary can afford to pay off the regular fees that come with them. If not, determine measures to have just one.

4 – It's a Sale, It's a Sale!

Take advantage of stores' sales. During one, you can avail of huge discounts. So, if you are thinking of buying that sofa for $400, check whether a sale is in order. Until then, put off your purchase. If you are lucky, that item will be yours for $200.

5 – A Long, Windy Road

Aim for long-term goals instead of living for the moment (paycheck to paycheck). Buy what you truly like (be it costly) in favor of what you can currently afford. Joy comes with achieving a goal, regardless of how small it is but the bigger the goal, the bigger the reward is.

6 – No to Gimmicky Insurance Deals

Avoid signing up for insurance gimmicks. Insurance agents may come to you with great deals such as accidental death double indemnity and short-term health insurance. Since they are usually expensive, say no to the temptation. While they could be promising, chances are, you would not need them and you would not benefit from them.

7 – On the Record

Keep track of all your typical expenses for food, transportation, and extras. Assess how much you usually spend each day. This way, you can start setting a limit for your daily expenses the following week.

8 - Just You

Focus on yourself, rather than focusing on something that another person possesses. For example, your neighbor bought a new phone. Instead of envying him, pay attention to your own wants and your own needs.

9 – The Whole and Not Just the Parts

Buy goods in bulk - especially ones you consume regularly such as rice, coffee, and powdered milk. For one, bulk-buying grants discounts. For another, you'll save on transportation cost.

10 – Save, Save, Save

Stop purchasing items you want but will not use. Be meticulous and avoid letting a cent go to waste.

Thanks for Previewing My Exciting Book Entitled:

"Frugal Simplicity: 101 Ways To Use Frugal Simplicity For Organizing And Decluttering Your Life And Embracing The Simplicity Lifestyle For Greater Personal Finances And Freedom!"

To purchase this book, simply go to the Amazon Kindle store and simply search:

"FRUGAL SIMPLICITY"

Then just scroll down until you see my book. You will know it is mine because you will see my name "Lilly Sparks" underneath the title.

Alternatively, you can visit my author page on Amazon to see this book and other work I have done. Thanks so much, and please don't forget your free bonuses

DON'T LEAVE YET! - CHECK OUT YOUR FREE BONUSES BELOW!

Free Bonus Offer: Get Free Access To The www.LuxyLifeNaturals.com VIP Newsletter!

Once you enter your email address you will immediately get free access to this awesome newsletter!

But wait, right now if you join now for free you will also get free access to the "Secrets of Becoming A Meditation Expert – In 7 Days!" free Ebook!

To claim both your FREE VIP NEWSLETTER MEMBERSHIP and your FREE BONUS Ebook on the SECRETS OF BECOMING A MEDITATION EXPERT IN 7 DAYS!

Just Go To:

www.LuxyLifeNaturals.com